Get Happy

& Confident

A No-Nonsense Guide to

Happiness, Self-Esteem and charisma

Contents

"Life is essentially sad. Happiness is sporadic. It comes in moments and that's it. Extract the blood from every moment."
—Robert Redford[1]

---

[1] Published in the January 2011 "Meaning of Life" issue (Esquire)

This book contains general reference information and is not intended as a substitute for consulting with your physician. Neither the publisher nor the author assumes any responsibility for any adverse effects that may result from your use of this book. I am not a doctor, and I do not give any medical or psychological advice in this book. If you suspect you have a medical problem, we urge you to seek medical attention from a competent health care provider.

I want to thank all the clients who gave me permission to publish their stories in the hope that they will help you.

Before We Start

Thank you for starting this special journey. While it may be difficult to imagine right now, this book will be the first domino that starts the change you've been seeking.

That's quite a statement, I know, but it's true. I will show you how to get confident and happy. It will be an amazing journey, and I hope that you are excited. As I'm writing this book for you, I am excited about the changes this book will initiate in your life.

Happiness is a state of mind that you deserve, and you can achieve it.

Happiness is a choice.

Being confident is linked to being happy in a strong way.

I wish you the best of luck!

Who Am I?

Why on Earth Should You Listen to Me?

I have an important question: what would make you happier? If you could change or have anything, what would make you happier?

Is it:

- a soul mate

- more money

- a better job

- better looks

- better health

- freedom

What is it for you?

Before I wrote this book, I did an extensive survey and asked everyone who was on my mailing list (around eighty thousand people at the time) what would make them happier. The list above includes the top six responses.

The real question is this: will any of those things truly make you happier? Science shows they will for a short time, but it won't be lasting happiness. Because I presuppose that you are looking for lasting happiness, you'll have to look somewhere else. The important conclusion is that most people want to be happier; they are trying to achieve things and do things that will make them happier. The problem is that most people are looking in the wrong places and are spending valuable time and money on stuff that won't provide durable and lasting happiness.

The goal of this book is to help you look in the right places. What is also important is that I don't claim to be a know-all. I want to give you the tools and techniques that have worked for me and for my clients, and I hope that you will use them. That's the only way to see what will or won't be powerful for you.

My name is Geert, and I'm from Brussels, Belgium. For fourteen years, I had severe panic attacks, agoraphobia, fear of driving, fear of flying, social phobia, fear of getting sick, anxiety, and stress. These panic attacks and anxieties limited my life to such an extent that I never left my house. That was not fun.

In 2004, I finally found a solution for my problems, and I started to help other people by creating a CD course and a website called ilovepanicattacks.com.

In 2011, after helping literally tens of thousands of people overcome their panic attacks, I decided to write this book.

Panic attacks are an obvious limitation to life, but there are more sneaky obstructions and obstacles that can take the fun of life away.

How many things do you not do because of a lack of self-esteem? How many decisions did you not make?

What's the first thing you think when you wake up? "YES, another day of fun!" Something else?

Throughout the day, do you feel energized? Do you thrive?

It's my belief that many people are living their life, but only a few of them thrive, enjoy it, and get the most out of it.

I know, because I've been there. During the panic attack period in my life and even after, I had low self-esteem.

When I was in a group of people, I didn't know how to communicate. Some people took advantage of that. They saw that I wasn't that confident and that I felt "less" than them.

Some people will try to use you, not because they are bad, it's just because they can. It's time to put an end to this.

I've had to change the way I think to overcome some of those self-esteem issues, and the techniques gave me amazing results. My clients have been using them for a couple of years as well. You'll read about their stories.

If and when you use the techniques I'll describe, you'll see that your social status will start to change. There's no need to buy new items like a fancy car or shoes—the way you react and act will need to change.

I've transformed the way I look at my life and see the world. Many people pursue happiness but never find it. I'm not saying that it is easy, but there are techniques that you can use to simply be genuinely happy. You will feel different. Happiness is a feeling.

Low self-esteem and anxiety are like a virus. They start to control more and more aspects of your life. Maybe you've seen this virus in action in someone's life.

The good news is that happiness and confidence are potent, little and smiling viruses as well. They will spread throughout your life and if you master happiness, you'll see changes in each and every area of your life: your personal life, your professional life, your relationships, your finances, and so on.

Everything will be affected. This is not a miracle but because of the way you see the world and react to it.

Would you like to see what can change in your life?

Let's get started.

"Damn You, Low Self-Esteem"

The Things that Never Were

Erica had a problem. She knew she could do so much more with her life, but she didn't know where to start. She felt "less" than other people. She was afraid to be assertive or to take the lead. Because of this, she missed out on great career moves, and in her personal relationships, people couldn't see her true value because she was afraid to show who she really was. This alone made her unhappy, and she felt as if she was missing out on something. She was.

Brian discovered something amazing. When he surfed around on social network sites and read the status updates, it seemed that everybody was living a great life. They all seemed so happy, and their lives seemed so perfect. Was this a charade or was it true? Were they really that happy? How did they do it?

Sarah had forgotten how to be happy. She was living her life, taking care of the daily chores, doing her thing. She had lost her smile ages ago. She was thirty-seven and since she passed twenty-one, when true responsibility came knocking at the door, she forgot how to smile. She thought that people didn't really like her, especially at work. She sometimes felt left out and had a hard time communicating with a specific group of colleagues. They always ate lunch together, yet she was never invited.

Rachel had everything she wanted: a house in the suburbs, a nice paycheck at the end of every month, a husband, and two children. There was only one problem: Rachel wasn't happy. Every day felt the same. Was she really alive? She realized that something was missing, even though she "had it all". She wasn't happy and wanted to change that.

These are the stories of a few of the people I've been able to help over the years.

As you can see in every story, low self-esteem or not being confident acts like a handbrake on life. You move ahead but not at optimal speed, and there will be resistance.

People who are not happy walk through every day. They never stop and enjoy what they are doing. Isn't that what life is supposed to be about?

Why where these people like this?

The secret behind the method that I will show you in this book is to first look at the causes—then at what to do about them. As long as the causes are present, something will drag you down. We need to cut you loose first.

Are you up for it?

I hope so!

Who Are You?

Who Would You Like to Be?

If you randomly picked one hundred people that you came in contact with the past two weeks and asked them who they thought you are, what would their responses be?

People respond to you according to the image you portray of yourself.

Let's look at this girl:

How do you feel about her?

Who is she?

Is she self-confident?

Is she happy in life?

Do you think she has a great boyfriend or husband?

Is she attractive?

How will other people react to her if this is the face she usually puts on?

As humans, we are instinctively able to "paint an entire picture" of who someone is with the blink of an eye. That's why first impressions are important. In fact, every impression is important.

If you've taken the time to answer my questions about her, you have an idea of who she is. Your mind filled in the blanks.

Great. Let's look at the following picture.

How do you feel about her?

Who is she?

Is she self-confident?

Is she happy in life?

Do you think she has a great boyfriend or husband?

Is she attractive?

How will other people to react to her if this is the face she usually puts on?

I think you know where I'm going at with this. Although it's the same girl, people respond in a totally different way to her. This version of her will be found more attractive, happier, and with at least a decent level of self-confidence.

In a sense, it doesn't matter what other people think about her (or about you), but how people react to her does matter.

We humans are emotionally and socially intelligent. Not so long ago, we tended to live in groups of people, in packs, and it was important to quickly know who was dangerous and might kill us, who the leader was, etc.

Within a couple of seconds after meeting someone, we had to be able to immediately know who we were dealing with, because back then our life depended on it.

We still have this system, and we fill in the gap of uncertainties we don't know about the other person. This is why a first impression is important.

If you want to be happy and confident in what you do, it's crucial that you get this.

This is a vicious cycle. If you don't feel happy and don't exude self-confidence, people will treat you differently. Some will take advantage of you, and therefore you might

find reasons why indeed you shouldn't be happy or have a lot of self-confidence.

People always fill in the blanks. We all do.

If I tell you that I flew from Brussels to Los Angeles last week and had trouble finding my luggage, what's the image you get? You probably start to think about an airport, airplanes, the luggage belt, etc. Who says I didn't travel on a hot air balloon or something else?

You just filled in the blanks. People quickly decide who you are, fill in the blanks, and act accordingly.

For instance, if you hear a remark from a colleague and react in an aggressive way, you've just shown that colleague how to get to you. You've shown your weakness. That colleague might take advantage of you from then on because you've positioned yourself "below" him or her.

That's funny, right?

People may see one behavior and start to treat you differently *if* you allow them to.

Your emotions are in a "control room" in your head, and that control room has some hidden doors. Once you show one of those doors to someone else, the other person can come in and control your emotions.

If they get through the door, they can make you feel good or bad. I'm sure you've had this happen to you—someone knew exactly how to make you happy, while someone else knew exactly how to make you feel bad.

Don't Depend on Others

One way to be happy and self-confident is to cut yourself loose from that behavior. Don't let others decide how and what you feel.

Let me give you an example. You're walking through the neighborhood, and a group of people in their twenties pass by you. The second they're behind you, they all start to laugh out loud.

What were they laughing about?

What would you think they were laughing about? You?

That's what most people would think. When they think this, they feel bad or sad for minutes, hours, or days. Why?

Let's look at the options.

A. **They were laughing with you** (not probable).

Suppose they were laughing with you. That's not a nice thing to do, so why would you allow "bad people" to control your emotions and how you feel about yourself?

Wouldn't it be better if only the people you love and who love you get to do that?

You can always make this choice. You might still get the initial reaction and bad feeling, but you can reason with yourself and say, "I don't know or like those people, but they shouldn't control how I feel, so whatever they think, it's okay."

I know this is easier said than done and will require some practicing, but it will be worth it. I sincerely hope that you will give it a try on multiple occasions and in multiple situations.

B. **They were not laughing with you** (probable).

This is the probable option, and it's even worse. They were not laughing with you, but you still chose to feel bad about yourself and have a bad day.

We do this all the time by the way, but my goal is to give you the power of choice.

The next time that you feel a sad or bad feeling or your self-confidence drops, check out *why* you had it and then decide if you want to allow that person to control your feelings.

Most people lose a lot of energy trying to be liked by people they don't like. Those people are not worth your energy or efforts.

Someone with true self-confidence doesn't depend on the opinion of others.

Think about your favorite American president. Presidents are both liked and hated. Those groups of people have always existed, and yet your favorite president exuded confidence, right?

Your favorite president felt good about himself. Regardless of what others thought, he was there to accomplish a goal, a mission, and that's what he was going for. He did not depend on others to be self confident and/or happy.

How would your life change when you decide "I'm going to be self-confident from now on; I'm going to accomplish my missions in life, the things I find important, regardless of what other people think!"?

I had panic attacks for fourteen years and found a way to overcome them. Because it worked so well for me, I decided to help others by creating a CD course.

When I had decided to do this, I told my friends, parents, and family. They all said, "Really? You're not a psychologist, so who is going to listen to you?" They advised me not to do it. If I had allowed them to get me off track, I wouldn't have started.

I decided to continue and recorded the first version of my CD course in Dutch (my native language). The first email I got from someone who was interested was full of hate: "What? You've had this for yourself and now you ask money for your solution? You should give it away for free and share it with the world, etc."

I could have let myself be influenced by that person. She had a point, but I didn't choose the society we live in. If I didn't get paid for my time, I couldn't buy food, I would end up living on the street and I couldn't help anyone.

I was on a mission and didn't allow her to control my emotions.

Many years later, my CD course has been translated into three languages and has helped tens of thousands of people, all over the world, to overcome their panic attacks.

I've had experiences I would have never imagined possible because of this.

Why? Because I had a mission and did not allow others to make me feel bad. Only *I* was allowed to make me feel bad.

What are the things you would like to do in your life, things that might make you happy but you don't do them because of negative remarks from others, lack of self-confidence, or something else?

Please remember this quote: "Most people regret *not* having done something; they don't regret the things they did."

What is your mission? Why are you here on this earth, and are you living up to your potential?

Your Mission and Movie Stars

I've had the luck to meet some movie stars in the past couple of years through the coaching programs I create. Most of them are great people when they're not in the spotlight.

They are a special breed of people to me. They get rejected a lot, but they are on a mission, and they do not give up.

There's one man, for instance, who played in a couple of movies featuring a boxer. He was rejected many times when he was first trying to become an actor. He heard comments like "You are ugly, NEXT," and "Learn English." That man became a big movie star because he didn't give up.

Some people might feel bad when they hear those comments, but he didn't let it get to him. He was on a mission and knew that he could only fail the day he stopped trying.

What is your mission? Why are you here on earth? Take some time to think about this. Fill in the blanks below:

"When I'm ………., I feel so happy."

"When I …………, I feel so happy."

That's your mission. If you are not doing something with your mission, now is a good time to start. Include it in your activities.

There's nothing that will make you feel more fulfilled, happy and self confident than that!

Please, don't just read this and continue. Stop, take a second, let it sink in, find your mission, and decide what steps you can take to include it in your life.

It's Not in Your Genes

Some people love to blame their genes for the problems they face. It makes everything easier, because it relieves them of any form of responsibility. They believe they can't change the problems, but they are wrong. There are indeed some things programmed in your genes that cannot be changed, but there is much that you can change.

Did you blame your genes for a behavior? What if they accounted for only 50 percent to 60 percent of what you are or how you feel? What if you had control over the rest? Would you be willing to give it a shot?

When I had panic attacks and was depressed, many of the doctors and psychologists I met stated that I would have to learn to live with them and that I would have to be on medication for the rest of my life. I am so happy that I never accepted those claims.

I was able to change my feelings and the mental problems I was facing. I not only overcame serious panic attacks and agoraphobia but also found ways to be truly happy!

They never told me that I could feel different if I were willing to change certain habits and to do certain things on a daily basis to feel that happiness and confidence. One example is to smile more. I consciously smile more, especially when I face personal or professional challenges. It sounds too easy, yet so few people do this. It's not all that I do but is one example.

Most people know that they have to put in effort when they want a physical thing or a change (when they want to lose weight, learn how to drive a car, learn how to swim, and so). Most people don't know that you can learn how to feel a certain way as well, all you have to do is to put in an effort. Try the techniques in this book, and find out which ones work best for you.

What You Should Remember after This Chapter:

✓ If you act unhappy and as if you have low self-esteem, people will treat you in a different way; because of this alone, you might feel unhappy and less confident. It is a vicious cycle.

✓ People fill in the blanks. They decide who you are based on how you act.

✓ Some people try to be liked, even by people they don't even like themselves. This is a waste of time and energy.

✓ Some people try to hold you down and have their own personal agenda when dealing with you. Do what matters for you, and don't seek the approval of others.

What You Should Try after This Chapter:

✓ Find out who you are. Play with the way that people react to different versions of you. For example, if you never smile and say hello, try it. When you lock eyes with a stranger, smile and say hello. If you always dress in black, try different colors. If you always sound nervous when you talk, talk slowly during conversations and take your time. Change small variables like these. Find out how people react in different ways when they *see* a different version of you.

✓ Make a mental note every time you are worried about what other people think about you and especially when you let it control your decisions or feelings. This might seem contradictory to the first exercise, where you play with what other people think about you, but that's the goal. What other people think won't matter any longer when you learn that their opinion will change the minute you change a small variable.

✓ Think about your mission. What makes you happy (things you do, have, see, etc.)?

Anxiety and Your Ego

Why Those Two Love Each Other

Maggie always wanted to do great things. She wanted to become a singer, and she had a great voice. Her parents discouraged this and told her about all of the singers who were broke and having trouble making ends meet.

One friend questioned Maggie's looks: "Don't you have to be thin and beautiful to make it as a singer?". Maybe she wasn't really a friend after all.

Her school had tryouts for a school play when she was in her last year. She had been practicing a lot, but the week before the tryouts, she started to feel anxious. "What if my parents are right? There's no future in this, so why am I doing it? I don't look as good as I should. People might laugh at me, and what if I forget my lines?" Maggie decided to listen to her ego, which was looking for the safe route with no pain or anxiety. She cancelled her tryout, thus giving up on what made her truly happy and fulfilled.

Although Maggie was always singing in the shower and training her voice to perfection, she got scared. It was true that she wasn't skinny and she wasn't the most beautiful girl in school. She decided to forget about singing and focus on her school work.

That would be the safe solution.

Maggie got her degree and she got a job as a saleswoman for a pharmaceutical company. She made good money and thought she had made it. She drove an expensive German car, had people looking up to her, and got a lot of approval from her parents and the people around her.

There was only one problem. She wasn't happy, she wasn't fulfilled and still did not have a lot of self-esteem.

One day, her car broke down, and she had to drive around in an old Chevrolet for a couple of hours. She felt that all people were looking at her and wondering why she was in "that ugly car." (Nobody was looking, but she imagined that they were.)

During the recession, she lost her job and her status.

It hit her, as hard as a fly hits a windshield when it decides to cross over the freeway on a dark night without wearing reflective gear.

She had always done what other people would approve of and avoided everything that people might disapprove. She avoided everything that made her insecure or anxious.

What if that was the reason she wasn't happy?

She decided to get off the road she was on and pick a different road, just to see what it would change.

Maggie started to sing again. She started to sing in small restaurants and bars and worked her way up. I met her in one of those restaurants, and she told me her story.

She made less money than before, but she's never been happier because for the first time she said, "Whatever happens, it's okay. Let's try this."

Most people are born to depend on others. It's in our nature. When we are young, we are controlled by ego and anxieties.

These will try to control you when you are an adult, but don't let them.

Your ego is a part of you; it's trying to make sure that everything is perfect. Here's what it is looking for:

- **Every day should be the same as the last one**. Change is bad. Your ego doesn't want you to leave your comfort zone, because new territories might be dangerous. When everything stays the same, at least nothing bad can happen (even though you will be deprived of happy moments as well).

- **People need to like and love me.** Your ego feels lonely and has learned to depend on others. When you were a baby, this was vital for your survival. Just suppose nobody loved you when you were born…well nobody would feed you and you wouldn't be here today. Babies learn quickly how to be liked by others. They make a funny face, and the adults say, "Ooooh, look at that cute little baby." Babies learn how to get attention, because they need it.

Some adults are still looking for this attention and need it, just like food, to feed their ego. When they don't get compliments about their looks or something they've done, they feel bad. They don't know how to compliment themselves or not need the approval of others. Their ego is still controlling them. I've been there. This book will help you to change that situation.

- **The ego is super anxious**. Your ego doesn't want you to take risks. If you let your ego control you, you would be living in a castle with guards, with everything you need so you would never have to come out. Nothing could hurt you physically (tigers, bees, dragons) or emotionally (love interests, job opportunities, risks you want to take but might not succeed in). That's the only way your ego can make sure you survive.

Is that a happy and fulfilled life?

When you feel anxious, love it. Anxiety means that you are living or are about to do something that will make you sad OR happy.

The biggest risk in life is not taking one.

When you're standing at the top of a ski slope, you might feel anxious. What you are about to do is dangerous. You might break a leg, or you might get a great adrenalin rush and a "yeehaw!" feeling you'll still remember years from now.

Are there things you want to do but you don't because you're afraid that things might turn bad?

They can, but that's life. To enjoy the sun, you need to know what rain is. Do not let your ego decide what you do or don't do.

When I had anxiety attacks and agoraphobia, I did not have a life for fourteen years and avoided a lot. There are a lot of experiences I should have had as a teenager but never had. That's why when I feel anxious now about something I want to do, I *have to* do it. The anxiety means that I could have a super duper experience! Because I'm still alive, happy, and confident when I write this, none of the choices I've made have destroyed anything that couldn't be fixed.

What are the choices you should make? The decisions you've pushed back because you are unsure about them, you procrastinated, or you were anxious?

Try them. Even a bad experience is an experience, and life is a series of experiences. Even the bad ones are great if you grow from them.

One method I used to overcome my fears is the phrase, "Whatever happens, it's okay." That phrase has changed my life more than anything else, and I hope it will change yours as well.

"Whatever happens, it's okay" is the antidote to anxiety, unhappiness, and low self-esteem.

Life has many options, many moments. Some will be extremely gratifying and will make you so happy that you'll feel an energy you can feel only a few times in a lifetime. Other moments will make you so sad that you won't know where to crawl. To feel those happy moments, risk feeling the bad ones.

Anthony Robbins said (and I'm paraphrasing), "If you want to avoid the fall from high to low, you can only live in the lows."

Because you're reading this book, I assume that you don't want to live in the lows.

How do you feel about this? Are you already taking risks in life, doing things that give you an anxious feeling but that make you feel great when it works out?

This is one of the secrets to happiness and confidence.

The "whatever" attitude helps to build your self-esteem as well. How many things would you do if outcome didn't matter? When do you feel the limits of your self-confidence?

Now imagine that you didn't care that the worst you could imagine actually happened! Would that change your self-confidence?

When you truly accept that whatever happens, it is all okay, there can be no fear and no self-confidence issues.

You can truly be *yourself* and live the way you should live. You try new adventures in life. Some work out well, others don't, and that's all okay. It was still a great day.

This might sound a little strange, but I live this way as much as I can. I consciously put myself on the "whatever" track when I start to drift, but so much has changed in my life since I changed my thinking.

I'll give you a technique to live more like this in the next chapter.

What You Should Remember after This Chapter:

✓ Feel what your ego is. Recognize when it wants to take over control, when it wants things to be the same and without risks.

What You Should Try after This Chapter:

✓ When you find ego-resistance, try whatever it is afraid of anyway (unless, of course, it is physically dangerous). If you don't feel like going to a party because you won't know anyone, go anyway, have fun, and leave whenever you want. The biggest risk in life is not taking one.

The "I Have One More Month to Live" Technique

What a Winning Lottery Ticket Can Do

Did you see the movie *The Bucket List* with Morgan Freeman and Jack Nicholson? It portrays what I'm about to describe. Here's the storyline in short: Corporate billionaire Edward Cole and working-class mechanic Carter Chambers have nothing in common except for their terminal illnesses. While sharing a hospital room together, they decide to leave it and do all the things they have ever wanted to do before they die—everything on their "bucket list." In the process, they heal each other, become unlikely friends, and ultimately find joy in life.

They start to live and feel happy right before they are supposed to die.

It doesn't have to be that way, and you can start living this way whenever you want. Sometimes it helps to trick your mind.

Did you ever notice how when you have a fixed deadline, it's hard to motivate yourself until you think that you'll never make it? Something kicks in, and you're able to do things you didn't believe were possible in that timeframe.

In a way, this is what happens in this movie. The two men have only so much time to live, and they then think about all the things they should have done and do them!

Why start when you're dying? Why start next week?

Why not start right now?

True happiness can be found in doing the things you love as much as you can. I don't know what they are for you, but the funny thing is that most people don't know what they are for themselves.

Do you know?

If you only had one month to live, what would you do?

Would you care about what other people thought? Would you not do certain things out of anxiety? If the anxiety vanished, would you do them?

It's all about perspective.

Let me give another rather example. You are standing on a sailboat and looking at the water. There are three white sharks swimming around in circles. You wonder why they do that. They're not in a fish bowl, right? They have the entire ocean and yet they swim around you in circles. Would you be afraid to sit in an inflatable lifeboat in the water at that time? You would still be in a boat but a lot closer to those pearly whites.

Now, let's imagine someone planted a powerful bomb in the boat that is set to detonate in thirty seconds. Would you jump and sit in the life boat?

You won't even hesitate. The bigger anxiety took over and made the smaller one (the sharks) go away.

You see this in some movies. Something bad is about to happen (an explosion, for instance) and it's too late to run away, and the male and female lead kiss for the first time.

Why only then? Anxiety and self-esteem issues can hold you back, but when the end is imminent, you would be surprised of what becomes possible.

All the *what if?* questions fall away. You do what you really want to do.

For the next couple of days, when you have a decision to make and you don't want to do something out of fear or because of a lack of self-confidence, ask yourself, "Would I do it if I only had one minute/hour/day/week/month to live?"

Whatever the answer is, do it.

Some example real-life experiences might include these:

- Should I go talk to that person?

- Should I go to that party?

- Should I take that job offer?

- Should I visit that country?

- Should I reconnect with someone I haven't seen in a long time?

- Should I do that stupid, funny thing again that made me so happy when I was a kid?

Most people regret the things they didn't do, not the things they did. Becoming confident and happy means living your life and doing things that make you happy, even at the risk of unhappiness.

Relationships are a great example. Some people don't want a relationship, they have been hurt before and refuse to feel that pain again. Because of this, they deprive themselves of the happy moments that a couple can have.

Another great technique is my "winning lottery number technique."

Say that you have to go to a reception alone and know that a lot of people will be there. How will you feel beforehand? Anxious? Maybe you won't know how to talk to those people, or you won't be radiant, happy, funny, and charismatic.

How would you feel if you just realized that you have a winning lottery ticket and have won a billion dollars?

Imagine this. Would you smile while walking into that reception? Would you be radiant, talkative, and full of self-confidence?

I've researched this issue and asked subscribers to my newsletter this question. Out of five thousand respondents, 4,765 claim they would feel full of self-confidence. That's 95.3 percent!

You don't even need the winning ticket. As we've seen, the mind doesn't know the difference between what's real and what we vividly imagine.

I've been using this trick for a couple of years, and it works wonders for me. I hope you will give it a try.

When you feel reluctant to do something, when you feel self-esteem issues, behave like you would with a real winning ticket in your pocket!

Amazing things might happen.

What You Should Remember after This Chapter:

✓ It's all about our thoughts. Our thoughts control how we feel. It's not the winning ticket that really changes everything; it's you, because you'll think in a new and different way.

What You Should Try after This Chapter:

✓ On a piece of paper, write WINNING LOTTERY TICKET and put it in your pocket. When stressed or unhappy, touch it, feel it, and think about winning the lottery. Then, for fun, act as if you did (but don't tell anyone).

✓ The problem is not that life is too short. It's that people wait too long before they start living it. This week, do one thing you've always wanted to do but keep postponing.

The Power of ;-)

What Your Smile Can Change

Do you smile a lot? Smiling has a profound effect on your happiness and your self-confidence.

Do happy people smile because they are happy, or does smiling make you happy?

Let's look at our test girl again:

How do you feel about her now?

Is she confident?

Is she attractive?

Would you like to be around her?

She has a neutral face here and will receive neutral reactions from the people she meets.

More importantly, she will not feel very happy. It is impossible for her to be happy with a facial expression like this.

Now look at the next picture:

This is still the same girl. Look at her for at least ten seconds. Focus on her face while you count to ten.

How did *you* feel?

Did it lift your mood? Would you like to be around her? Is this a confident girl?

You might have answered "yes" to those questions. Most people do, and that is the way nature intended it to be.

A smile is powerful, both for the person who smiles and for the people around him or her.

Do you know why the Mona Lisa got so much interest throughout history? What's so special about her? It's just a woman sitting in front of an unrecognizable background, and she's not really pretty, so why all the interest?

Because of her smile. She's offering a smile that intrigues most people. Is she happy? Is she sad?

In 2005, researchers Harro Stokman and Nicu Sebe used emotion recognition software on the painting to discover her emotions. Mona Lisa was found to be 83 percent happy, 9 percent disgusted, 6 percent fearful, and 2 percent angry.

A smile can fascinate us, and there are many reasons why a smile can make you happy and confident at the same time.

Why a Smile Can Make You Happy

You might have heard the phrase, "Smile and be happy." This issue has been researched extensively.

In 1988, a man called Fritz Strack conducted an interesting study. As is often the case, the participants didn't know what was being studied. They thought they were testing how people without arms or hands can still use things (for example, they had to use their mouth to control a pencil and write).

The participants had to use a pencil in two specific ways, and then they had to rate cartoons for funniness.

One group had to hold a pencil between their teeth, with both ends of the pencil sticking out of their mouth from left to right. (I invite you to try this and put a pencil between your teeth now.)

The second group had to put the pencil between their lips. This time, a part of the pencil was in their mouth, and the part they wrote with was sticking out. The pencil could not touch their teeth at all (only their lips). I invite you to try this.

In both cases, they had to then rate cartoons for funniness. Something remarkable happened.

People who did the first exercise (a pencil between the teeth, both ends of the pencil sticking out of the mouth) rated the cartoons as funnier than the members of the second group, who indicated that they themselves were actually happier. Happy people find things funny, and unhappy people don't think anything is funny.

When you put a pencil between your teeth, you are in a "smiling position" as if you are smiling, though you don't consciously know it. Because you activate those muscles, you automatically feel happier.

Many follow-up studies prove that smiling makes you happy. The next time you feel sad, decide to smile.

Why a Smile Can Make Others happy

Smiling also changes the way people around you feel. This is important for your social relationships and thus for your self-confidence. It's easier to have a lot of self-confidence when other people love being around you.

Swedish researchers Ulf Dimberg and Monika Thunberg did a study on rapid facial reactions to emotional facial expression[2] and found that seeing the picture of a happy face, when really studying it, pulls your own face into a smile.

If you looked closely at the smiling girl a couple of pages back, you should have felt an emotional change.

This is a "positive vicious cycle." When we see someone else smile, we might smile and because we smile, we feel happy ourselves. We often link this happy feeling to the smiling person. For "some unknown reason," we love being around the person.

If I ask you to think about the people you love being around, who are they? Are they depressed? Sad? Always complaining? Or are they happy, smiling people who enjoy life?

Happiness attracts and is contagious. For the next few days, when you make eye contact with other people, smile. Don't make it a Mona Lisa smile, where your true intentions are unclear, but a real smile.

---

[2] *Scandinavian Journal of Psychology* 39 (2000), pp. 39–46.

I hope you will try this. You'll be amazed of what will change. For one, most people will smile back.

When you genuinely smile at other people, you can make use of "the happy face advantage." Psychologist Jukka Leppänen and colleagues did a study to see what types of faces are easiest to recognize. Both the participants who were depressed and those who were not recognized a happy face quicker than a sad or a neutral face.

We are programmed to find happy people and to stay around them. If you smile at people, if you're a positive person, people love being around you. They are programmed to do so.

Your self-confidence should never be built on what other people think of you. It shouldn't matter, but we are social animals, and it is easier to be happy and confident when people like being around you. They will, in turn, make you happier.

A crucial factor is in play. Never try to please people just to get them to like you. Smile because smiling makes you happy, not just to make other people happy. That's a side effect.

Some people are unhappy and lack self-confidence because they do everything for other people but forget about themselves. This is why it is important to choose the people you surround yourself with wisely.

What You Should Remember after This Chapter:

✓ When you smile, you will feel happier. Others will love being around you, and that, in turn, will make you even more happy.

What You Should Try after This Chapter:

✓ Say "cheese" ☺ on a daily basis.

✓ Put a note on your calendar or a Post-it® on your mirror, and every time you look at it, regardless of how you feel, smile.

Choose Your Friends

Why Not Choosing Wisely Can Make Your Life Miserable

We are social creatures. We're not built to live alone on an island, and like it or not, other people will always influence us.

Imagine that you are walking in the street and you will pass a woman, in her thirties, wearing a colorful dress that moves around with the wind while she walks. As she comes closer, she makes eye contact with you and gives you a genuine smile.

This will impact you. You might smile back, but a short connection between you and her is certain. Her emotions were contagious.

Here's another piece of proof. Have you ever seen someone else yawn and you had to yawn yourself?

We are built to be emotionally connected to others.

This has a downside. Surround yourself with people who feel miserable, who are jealous, who don't like you, who need you because they can use you, and you will feel unhappy yourself. Daniel Goleman, who wrote a phenomenal book, *Emotional Intelligence,* and another one about social intelligence, calls this "the social brain." According to him, the social brain is continuously influenced by the people we surround ourselves with.

I'm sure you can find proof of this. When someone who is depressed calls you, you might feel empty and unhappy after the call. When someone near you is excited, you get excited.

When people around you are anxious, you get anxious as well. Imagine you're talking to our test girl, and she makes this face. Look at her for at least ten seconds.

You may have had the feeling that I have with this picture: slight anxiety. Even if you didn't get it, imagine that you are talking to her and all of a sudden she shows that expression. You would turn around to see what's going on, right? We are programmed to do that.

We mirror the emotions of other people, so the people you surround yourself with are extremely important for your well-being. Do they support what you do? Do they give you compliments or positive energy? What's their outlook on life? Are they positive or do they complain all the time? You will be affected by them.

Happiness Cannot Be Found or Pursued

Why So Many People Waste Their Time Trying to Find It

Many people are looking for happiness, as if it is something that can be found and will stay. Sadly, this is not the case. When I launched my anti-panic attack program, some people were frustrated that it took fourteen weeks to get through it. They were looking for a miracle solution, one that required no work—that doesn't exist. However, those who were willing to put in the effort got better week by week. It was a process, not an event, and when they finally lived without panic attacks, it lasted. They had a deep understanding of the mechanism behind it. They knew what to do and kept doing it.

What I explain in this book follows the same process. You will have to *do* and use the techniques I describe to get happier and gain confidence. The beginning will be the hardest. I will give you exercises and ask you to do things that won't feel natural to you. If you put in the effort, you will soon start to feel the first changes, and you will be able to maintain them because you will understand the system behind them. Achieving anything that is worthwhile— like happiness or self-confidence—is a process, not a single event.

Most people who are rich did not get rich overnight, people who lose weight don't do it overnight, and people who learn a foreign language don't do that overnight.

Being happy and confident demands effort, not only to achieve it but to sustain it as well.

There is a positive note. Did you ever have to push a large object, like a car? The first inch is the hardest, but once you get rolling, it wants to continue. It's the same when you are looking for happiness and confidence. The beginning will be the hardest.

Buying Happiness, Money, and Cosmetic Changes

Why I Still Love My Old BMW Z3 Roadster

From the age of ten, I had to wear really big glasses, and that always made me unhappy. In 2000, I switched to contact lenses, and although I had a lot of problems wearing them, they made my life easier in many ways.

In March of 2007, I developed an allergy to contact lenses, so I could not continue to wear them. This made me unhappy. I was extremely nearsighted, so without glasses, I couldn't even find my own glasses.

In May of that year, I underwent Lasik eye surgery. Seconds after the operation, I could see clearly now…and the rain was gone too. It was all sunshine, and I was truly happy.

The funny thing is I got used to living without glasses. It became my new normal state.

Marketers call this a *dissatisfier*. A *satisfier* is something that makes you happy when it's present, and a dissatisfier is something that makes you unhappy when it's not present. All satisfiers eventually become dissatisfiers.

Can you imagine how happy people were when cars were first installed with air conditioning? No more arriving with a wet back on a hot day! Air conditioning was a satisfier, and it made people happy, but it became a dissatisfier. Today, it's normal to have air conditioning in a car (it doesn't make anyone happy), but the lack of air conditioning would make most people unhappy.

This is also why cosmetic changes do not provide lasting happiness or self-confidence. People who change something by means of surgery might feel happy afterward, but they soon return to their normal state. Some then change something else while looking for a "happiness rush."

This is not the way to find lasting happiness.

Psychologists talk about *hedonic adaptation* (why things, newfound beauty, or money don't make us any happier).[3]

Humans are naturally built to adapt quickly to a changing environment. Did you ever buy a new car that you were looking forward to buying, but when you got it, you felt happier for about two weeks? We all fall into this trap. I recently had it with a big-screen TV. I had to have a fifty-inch flat screen TV, because I was sure I would enjoy my weekly movie night so much more. I would be able to see details and really feel what was going on. That TV had the desired effect for about a month, until I saw a fifty-five-inch TV in a friend's house. We adapt, and we always want more. This never works. I am not saying it isn't okay to buy things. I love material things, just don't buy them to find happiness. Happiness cannot be bought. It is within you, and you don't need any money to get it to the surface and enjoy it.

Hedonic adaptation does have consequences. Everything around you that makes you happy at first will eventually

---

[3] S. Frederick, G. Loewenstein, "Hedonic Adaptation" in *Well-Being: The Foundations of Hedonic Psychology* (New York: Russell Sage Foundation, 1999).

make you feel indifferent. That said, if you are willing to take control and not just let things be, you can change this.

When I was approaching eighteen, the year I could get my driver's license, I dreamed about a BMW roadster, the Z3. Coming from a family with modest means, I could not afford this kind of sport-convertible. Seven years later, I was in a position to buy a second-hand Z3, exactly in the color I had always thought of. Putting the key in the ignition for the first time and hearing the engine made me so happy; I recall the moment as if it was yesterday. When I drove out of the shop, I was a very happy man. I still have this car, many years later, and although I could afford a newer version of the roadster, I found a way to be truly happy with this car. In this case, the hedonic adaptation couldn't touch me.

Why? Because I didn't let it influence me. Every week or so, I stepped into my garage and looked at the car. I enjoyed its beauty and thought of all the great moments I'd had and can still have with it.

It's just a car, but I consciously chose to make more of it. Every time I drive that car, I feel happy.

I've chosen to focus on the positive, on the good moments, on that happy feeling.

Where in your life could you do the same?

Studies show that most people feel great the first years of their marriage, but then hedonic adaptation starts to settle in. Marriage becomes normal, not something they are extremely happy about. The happy couples who remain happy don't take what they have for granted. They make the time to go out on dates (with each other), they think about all the great moments they have together, and they focus on the happiness they bring.

The same goes for money. You know the saying, "Money doesn't make you happy"? It's true. Money makes life easier, but it doesn't make you happy.

Lottery winners are often reverting to the same financial level they were before they won. Even people who manage to not spend everything don't say that they are any happier than others.

Think about the many movie stars who seem to have it all—looks, money, a great job—but who are deeply unhappy and addicted to substances.

Happiness is within you. If you try the techniques I've presented, you will feel a change.

What You Should Remember after This Chapter:

✓ Every "new" thing can become boring unless you protect yourself from this effect.

✓ Don't try to buy happiness or self-esteem. It won't last.

What You Should Try after This Chapter:

✓ When you feel like buying something to "make you feel better," don't. Try the techniques I describe in the book instead. They should have more power to change your feelings than buying that "thing" would. Buying an experience that you share with people you love is okay.

Positive Thinking Is Not the Solution

Why Saying Thanks Is One of the Solutions

With one specific kind of positive thinking, you deliberately focus on the things that make you feel good. That's where gratitude comes into play. Being grateful has been scientifically proven to enhance mood and increase your happiness. It's a special kind of positive thinking, because you start to focus on the things that make you feel good. You relive the moments or experiences you've had that made you feel good.

This is not some type of "spiritual guru trick." There is scientific proof that supports this idea.

Given that gratitude appears to be a strong determinant of well-being, several psychological interventions have been developed to increase gratitude. Watkins and colleagues[4] had participants test a number of gratitude exercises such as thinking about a living person for whom they were grateful, writing about someone for whom they were grateful, and writing a letter to deliver to someone for whom they were grateful. Participants in the control condition were asked to describe their living room.

Participants who engaged in the exercise showed increases in their experiences of positive emotion immediately after the exercise, and this effect was strongest for participants who

---

[4] P. C. Watkins, K. Woodward, T. Stone, and R. L. Kolts, "Gratitude and Happiness: Development of a Measure of Gratitude, and Relationships with Subjective Well-Being," *Social Behavior and Personality* 31 (2003): 431–452.

were asked to think about a person for whom they were grateful. Participants who had "grateful personalities" to begin with showed the greatest benefit from these gratitude exercises.

One of the reasons I never found help with the psychologists who tried to treat me when I had panic attacks, was that they always wanted to talk about my past. They wanted to talk about the bad moments in my past, and talking about them made me relive them. This made me feel sad instead of happy.

Wouldn't it be more fun to focus on the good events in your life, the things that make you feel happy? That's where the gratefulness exercise comes into play.

EXERCISE

For the next six weeks, keep a diary. Pick one day each week when you can make time for yourself: prior to going to bed, during lunch, whenever you can have a few minutes of "nobody will bother me" time. When the time comes, take your journal and write what you're grateful about. You can write about objects and material things, about experiences, about anything.

Here's an example from my journal.

I'm grateful for the invention of the Internet, which allowed me to help tens of thousands of people all over the world. I'm grateful for the invention of Lasik surgery; I can see better than I ever could with glasses or contact lenses. I'm grateful for my trip to California three months ago. While standing at the end of the pier in Newport Beach, I saw some dolphins passing by.

Even while copying my notes to include them in this book, I relive those moments of happiness. Try the exercise once a week for six weeks.

Another reason that this process works so well is because you will force yourself to enjoy the now. Have you ever thought back to a time where everything was so good that you would love to relive it, but at the time, you didn't realize how good it was because you never stopped to be grateful?

This exercise will not only help with your happiness factor, it will also boost your self-esteem. There will be moments where you will be grateful for something you realized or did or for something someone else did for you. This is powerful stuff.

Human beings are naturally programmed to focus more on the bad than the good. We might as well start consciously focusing on the good that is happening.

Being grateful will also save you money. Think about my Z3. I often take a moment to sit in and look at my car. I'm grateful for having found it, and because of this, the need to buy a newer model goes away.

There are however a couple of important remarks. One is to keep gratitude fresh. You do not need to keep repeating the same items that made you happy every week. Add simple things that happened that day, for instance. Gratitude should not be limited to the moment when you write about it. If you avoided a traffic jam by taking an earlier exit, be grateful. Happiness can be found in the little things as well.

If someone helps you, be grateful, and show gratitude to the person who helped you even when you're not in the mood. What goes around always comes around, and when you express gratitude, when you thank people sincerely when they help you, and become a more positive person, amazing things start to happen to you. It will be a positive vicious cycle.

Who could you thank? Is there anyone in your life who did an amazing thing for you? Can you thank him or her by calling or writing an e-mail or letter?

Did you ever notice how unhappy, depressed people seem to have all the bad luck? This is no accident. Their outlook on life attracts "bad luck." Happy, grateful people, on the other hand, rebound quicker when something bad happens to them and, in general, they have more opportunities in life. Think about the happy and unhappy people you know. Do you find evidence that supports my theory? That's one of the reasons to do this exercise.

Every now and then, reread your gratitude journal, especially when you feel down. I used to write in a paper journal, but I've changed to an application that I can access from my Smartphone and computer. I always have it available to me to reread it or add notes.

What Are You Lookin' At?

How to Use Your Focus to Feel Happy

It was the summer of 2004. A lightning strike hit during a dry time, and as a result, a violent fire was attacking the Los Angeles area. Hundreds had to evacuate their houses and leave everything behind.

I watched the news and saw an important piece that changed my outlook on life. A news reporter spoke with a woman (let's call her Marge) who was allowed to go back to her home for the first time since the fire. Her house was gone. There was nothing left.

"What was that?" the reporter asked, pointing to a large area of melted metal. Marge said, "That was my collection of old sports cars I worked on during the weekends. They were not insured against this."

Something caught the reporter's eye. Marge wasn't crying, she wasn't upset, she wasn't depressed. She was stable and almost smiling.

When the reporter asked her about it, in an effort to make her show some emotions, Marge said, "Look, yeah, I lost everything, but will crying make everything come back? Will that turn back the time? No, it won't, so what I'm going to do is get back to work and build everything up again. What happened has happened, and it's time to move on."

Can you imagine this? Even when everything seemed lost, she was still happy and willing to get back up on her feet. Marge opened my eyes.

In the last chapter, I stated that positive thinking won't make you happy. That wasn't entirely correct. Positive thinking, the way most people think about it, won't work. If all is bad and you say, "All is good," or if you're not full of self-esteem and you say, "I am full of self-confidence," you won't find a big difference in your happiness or self-esteem.

However, looking for the positive in life, even in problems and bad events, will help you to feel happier. It's a matter of changing your perspective, and one man who knows how to do this is W. Mitchell.

W. Mitchell had a motorcycle accident in which the gas tank exploded, leaving him severely burned. You would think this was enough to be unhappy and lose self-confidence, but not for W. Mitchell. He decided to pick himself up and live life to the fullest. He then had a crash in a plane and was left paralyzed. One could think being paralyzed and still severely burned would be enough to be unhappy and lose self confidence. Not for W.Mitchell. Instead of focusing on the bad luck he had, he chose to change his perspective. Instead of focusing on the thousand things he could no longer do, he chose to focus on the ten thousand things he could still do and be grateful for them.

He became mayor of Crested Butte, Colorado, became a motivational speaker, and became friends with ex-President Bill Clinton, Anthony Robbins, and other well-known people.

Why was he happy and self-confident? Because he changed his perspective and chose to be happy.

If a man who is severely burned and paralyzed can be happy and full of self-confidence, is there any reason why you and I can't be? It's all about the choices you make.

Imagine a soldier stepping on a land mine and losing a leg. That soldier (let's call him Private Idaho) has a choice. Private Idaho can say, "Oh no! I've lost a leg, look at me, I won't be able to do this and that." For the rest of his days, he will never be happy.

Private Idaho has another option. He can say, "Wow, close one. I'm so glad I still have one leg left. At least I can still stand tall" I can assure you that he will be grateful and happy every single day.

Isn't that funny? He's living in the same situation, but because he changed his perspective, he will be happier, be more fun to be around, will have better relationships, and have more self-confidence.

I realize this sounds difficult, and I'm not going to try to convince you of the opposite. Looking for the good is hard at first, because it won't feel natural. Swimming or driving a car didn't feel natural at first either, right? Looking for the positive in bad situations is addictive, and once that you feel the benefits, you'll keep doing it. I never stopped.

EXERCISE

What are you unhappy about? What might be lowering your self-esteem?

Is there another way to look at it? Can you change your perspective? Think about it, and write it in your journal.

Have a go at it. Take something to write and analyze this for a second. Don't just say: "yeah sure, I'll do it later". Please do it now or you will forget.

What You Should Remember after This Chapter:

✓ What you give attention to determines how you feel. Focus on the bad, and you will feel bad. Focus on the good, and you will feel good.

What You Should Try after This Chapter:

✓ When something bad happens this week, force yourself and try finding something positive about that event.

The Power of Relating

Why This Is a Double-Edged Sword

Relationships are important—we're not meant to be alone. I'm not talking about romantic relationships. You can have a lot of friends, never be married, or have a partner, and still be a happy person, but few people who don't talk to anyone will truly be happy.

Relationships are also dangerous. They can make us unhappy and significantly lower our self-confidence.

Studies show that people who are in a good marriage are happier than people who are single[5]. Needless to say, people who are in a bad marriage or in a bad relationship are significantly unhappier than people who are single.

You might have noticed, throughout your life, that the same goes for friendships. There are nurturing friendships that make you feel happy and self-confident, and there are friendships that drag all the energy, happiness, and self-confidence out of you.

How can you tell the difference between a good and a bad friendship? Whom should you walk away from?

An interesting study took place a while back.[6] The goal of the study was to see the effect of a positive reaction (when

---

[5] Seligman, Martin E.P. "Authentic Happiness." Somon and Schuster. 2002.
[6] Shelly L. Gable, Harry T. Reis, Evan R. Asher, and Emily A. Impett, "What Do You Do When Things Go Right," *Journal of Personality and Social Psychology* 87 (2004): 228–245.

good news was shared) as opposed to a negative reaction (when good news was shared).

Imagine you just won fifteen thousand dollars and you want to share the news with your friends and family. How would they react? Would they be happy for you? Would they be jealous?

People who would react negatively when you share good news are not your friends. This might seem obvious, but it is an important factor in your happiness, well-being, and self-confidence.

When you have good news to share (such as you just had a promotion or you can travel to a beautiful country for free), the reaction of the people you share it with is important.

When you hear a jealous or negative remark, the other person is thinking, "Why does he get this and not me?" This person obviously doesn't care about you.

If the other person is glad for you, even if the person would have loved to get the same gift or experience, it means a lot. When the other person reacts positively, this means he is happy for you *and* thinks you have a positive relationship. Robert Cialdini, one of my favorite authors (and in my opinion, a smart man when it comes to psychology and marketing), calls this "basking in reflected glory." The other person can enjoy the fact that you will enjoy something, as if he will experience it for himself. This creates a sort of intimacy with you.

Why should you risk sharing good news with anyone? The study I mentioned showed that communicating positive events with others was associated with increased, daily, positive effects and well-being beyond the impact of the positive effect itself. The study showed that you will feel better when you share good news, and you will feel even better when the other person is happy for you.

There's an even more important reason to share good things: to weed out the people who do not deserve your attention.

Did you know that people who make negative remarks can significantly lower your self-esteem and happiness? Did you ever spend time with someone only to feel empty, mad, or down afterward?

Those people take your happiness away, and they do it by attacking you in little ways. They don't make it too obvious; they give a negative remark here and there to push you down.

Of course, the sun can't shine all the time. You will find disputes and negative moments in every relationship. But sometimes you know someone who can *never* be happy when good things happen to you.

Those people should be avoided. They don't mean well.

Sharing happy news will quickly expose them. That's why I'm not afraid to share news with my friends when something good happens to me.

How do you react when someone shares positive news with you?

Watch closely the next time this happens. Really listen and share in the joy that the other person feels. It will strengthen your relationship, and to be happy and confident on a full-time basis, you need strong relationships with people.

When Somebody Doesn't Like You

There will always be people who are not fond of you, and nothing you do will change their mind. I believe that's okay. Obviously, there will also be a lot of people who genuinely like you.

What about when somebody doesn't like you but you still must deal with them at work or at family dinners?

People who talk down on you and make negative remarks may seriously lack self-confidence. They try to crawl out of the dark hole they find themselves in.

Here is an example. You buy a new car, and you are happy about it. Person X sees this and says, "Wow, what an ugly car." He may not be this direct, but you get the point. Person X might be jealous, and by "talking you down," he feels better about himself.

Say that you know a group of people, and you are all on the same level (income, relationships and so on). When you start to rise—you earn more, have a new great relationship, or bought the coolest goldfish in the world—those people will feel that you are outgrowing them.

If they truly love you, they will continue to support you, but if Person X is one of them, he will try to hold you down by telling you how risky it is, why he doesn't like it, why this and that.

Why does he do that? He lacks self-confidence, and when he sees what you are achieving, it reminds him of how miserable he feels. He doesn't like that feeling.

Do you know any bad people who talk loud at parties, who try to get attention, sometimes by badmouthing other people? People who try to control you?

If you can, avoid those people. They are not your friends. If you cannot avoid them, have pity for them. They feel bad about themselves and are using a childish approach to feel better. They want to bring you down to their level.

I'm sure you know people like this, but I hope you can use a different perspective, keep your own confidence together, and not let them touch you or your happiness.

That brings me to another important note. I used to hate certain drivers. I don't know if you've ever driven a car in Europe, but Europeans are very aggressive when driving. Europe is still my primary place of residence, so I drive there a lot.

When someone did something unfair toward me, like not stopping when the person should to let me through, I got mad. I've even shown the finger (yeah, I'm not proud of it).

Maybe you've done this as well. At that time, you felt your heart racing and your blood boiling.

What happened is I let that other driver, who has no respect for me, decide how I feel. I let him control my emotions.

How often does it happen that you ponder something someone said to or about you, or how someone treated you? Does it make you feel bad or unhappy? Does the other person deserve to have control over your feelings? I don't think so.

This is a big secret to personal happiness. I do not allow other people to control how I feel, especially not when I believe the other person doesn't even know or like me.

When my sister, whom I love, said something that hurt me, I accepted the feeling and saw what I could do to fix the problem. I knew that she loved me, so if she hurt me, there must be a legitimate reason.

When someone who is jealous of you, doesn't like your new-found confidence or happiness, or doesn't even know you does something that makes you feel bad, does the person deserve to control your feelings?

He doesn't. Think about what I describe here, and it will help you to get your smile back and feel happy again. Let it pass.

Confidence Breeds Confidence

What the Eiffel Tower Has to Do with This

Do you know the Eiffel tower?

I'm sure you do. Well I have a funny story about the Eiffel tower.

In May of 1925, a couple of the most successful dealers in scrap metal where attending a secretive meeting. They didn't even know what it was about before they arrived. The meeting took place in the most luxurious hotel in Paris, and they were to meet the deputy general of the Ministry of Post and Telegraphs.

When the gentlemen arrived, the deputy director, Monsieur Lustig, welcomed them in the beautiful suite. The men were impressed.

Lustig explained that the matter was urgent and required complete secrecy. He told the men, "The government will tear down the Eiffel Tower."

The dealers were stunned. Lustig explained that the Tower was meant as a temporary structure, and because the maintenance costs were so high, the government decided to tear it down and sell the metal.

Lustig told the men that they were all asked to make an offer on all the metal. He gave them secretive sheets with all the details of the Tower, including the weight, the amount of metal, etc. He included the amount of money they could make when they sold the metal to their clients.

He then guided the businessmen to a limousine and took them on a special tour on the Tower. At the end of the visit, he gave them four days to prepare an offer.

On the fifth day, each dealer made an offer, and Monsieur P. was the winner. To seal the deal, he had to transfer a check with a 25 percent down payment. The check was worth 250,000 francs (a little over $1,000,000 in today's currency).

When Monsieur P. arrived at the suite to hand over his check, he started to have doubts. He thought, "Why is this meeting in a hotel, if it is official business from the government?" He considered backing out.

Upon entering the room, Lustig greeted him and they had a talk. Lustig complained about his salary, about how hard it was to work for the government and not be paid enough. He was asking for a bribe.

Monsieur P. was delighted, as this took away his fear. It was clear that Lustig was working for the government. Every government official he had ever done business with had asked for a bribe.

Monsieur P. handed over the check and added several high-figure bills as bribe. In return, he received all the documents and the bill of sale.

He left the hotel as a happy man, dreaming about all the money he was going to make.

A couple of days later, he still hadn't heard from the government on what to do next. He called the office and asked to speak with deputy director Lustig.

The government had never heard of Lustig and confirmed the Eiffel Tower was not for sale.

He had been seriously conned.

This is an amazing story. It has everything to do with confidence.

Can you imagine what a confident man, a con artist extraordinaire, Lustig must have been?

Had he tried to sell a small building somewhere, no one would have believed him. He selected the tallest building in Paris and acted confident. The business men had believed every word he said.

Why is this? Because the emotion of confidence cannot be seen, only the acts of confidence.

When you act and look confident, you begin to feel more confident, and other people will see you as more confident.

People are always looking for leaders, for people they can follow. They look for confident women and men, and they will always be attracted to them. People don't gravitate toward people who cannot make up their minds, who are unsure, who cannot decide. Those people don't exude confidence.

We instinctively like the person who knows what he wants and acts as if he expects to get it.

If you're not full of confidence but want to be, "fake it 'til you make it."

If and when you act as if you have a lot of self confidence, others will treat you like someone with a lot of self confidence.

This is a natural instinct of humans. Do you remember the smile exercise earlier? Did you test it?

A confident person smiles a lot, and when you start smiling, even when you don't feel like it, people respond to you in a great new way.

Take a few minutes, and write down a list of at least ten people you know who have a lot of self confidence. Who is on your list?

Why are these people so confident?

How can you be sure? Did you use a lie-detector to make sure? Can you read their thoughts? Why do you think they are so confident?

It's because they *act* confident. If you want to be perceived as someone with a lot of confidence, act confident.

You might be skeptical and think, "I don't want to act, I just want to be." As always, please bear with me and just try it for a couple of weeks. Things that might feel unnatural to you now will become natural after a while. When you act confident, you'll start to feel confident for many reasons, one of them being that other people will treat you like a confident person.

Don't Hesitate

Confident men and women don't hesitate. They walk like they have somewhere to go, like they are going toward a goal.

When you're at a party, you can see this in action. People lacking self-confidence hesitate, move with hesitation, and try to stay under the radar, or they will do the opposite and be loud.

Confident people move around with determination. They move to a certain group of people, shake hands, and introduce themselves without hesitation.

The next time you're at a reception or party where most people don't know each other, try to observe how confident people walk and move their bodies.

When you move, move with determination, like you have a purpose.

Speak Slowly

Your voice shows how you feel, and other people respond to it. For example, the Speech Research Unit of Kenyon College proved that when someone is shouted at, he cannot help but shout back, even when he can't see the speaker.

This means that when you are angry and start to shout, the other person will instinctively become angry and shout back.

When you speak slowly and calmly, with determination, you will be seen as a charismatic person, and the person you talk to will often feel calm and at ease.

Speaking rapidly is a sign of nervousness and insecurity, but talking slowly portrays you as someone with confidence.

Eye Contact

People who don't make eye contact are less confident, people who stare and make eye contact continuously are creepy. People who are not afraid to make eye contact and divert their eyes briefly every couple of seconds are confident.

Smile Even When Attacked

Nothing conveys confidence more than a smile. If you did the smile exercise earlier, you've already seen the effects.

When someone attacks you in an emotional way, by giving a negative remark or that is intended to hurt you, don't respond, just smile.

I talked about not giving another person the key to the room where your emotions are controlled. If someone tries to hurt you with words and you react in an aggressive or angry way, the person knows that he reached your emotional-control room, and he knows how to get to you.

If you smile and say something like, "Yeah, that might be the case," you returned the "grenade," and it will hurt the person.

Imagine that someone says to Caroline, "Caroline, I don't like your hair," and Caroline says, "What? That really hurts! Why would you say that??" She has just shown that she depends on the opinion of others. Although this is human, someone with great self-confidence depends only on himself.

Imagine Caroline smiles and says, "Yeah, that might be the case," or "Interesting." Can you imagine the look on the other person's face? The "grenade" just bounced back.

This is a great example of not letting others control how you feel.

What You Should Remember after This Chapter:

✓ Other people won't automatically think you have great self-esteem. They will believe it when you act like someone with a lot of self-esteem (regardless of your own feelings). They can't read your thoughts, only your body language.

What You Should Try after This Chapter:

✓ Play with this chapter. When someone you know tries to hurt you, react differently than you would have in the past. Smile and make a joke out of it (even if it hurts).

✓ Play with your body language, and see how you feel and how others react. Always act as if you have a purpose.

The First Impression

What You Can Learn from Door-to-Door Salesmen

First impressions create a halo effect (a cognitive bias where one trait or one impression colors the entire impression we have of a person or company).

As an example, when you go to a restaurant and you're not treated well, you probably think the food doesn't taste good either. Your feelings spread.

First impressions count when you want to get something done from other people. Back in the day when salesmen went from door to door to sell vacuum cleaners, the unsuccessful ones said, "I'm sorry, I hope I'm not bothering you, but can I show you our new...." The housewife probably said, "I'm too busy, leave me alone." The salesman made the wrong first impression by apologizing before he even started his pitch. The more successful ones said, "Good afternoon. I have something with me that will help you to clean your house seventeen minutes quicker than it takes you right now. Can I come in?" They sold many more vacuums.

They made a strong, self-confident first impression.

You are more responsible for how people will respond to you than anything else. You create the first impression. If you act like you are a "nobody," people will think you are a nobody.

Do you know Donald Trump? Do you know the Trump buildings all over the world? That man has quite a presence.

Some people hate him, others love him, but he has a good presence, and he's full of self-confidence.

Imagine that someone wiped your memory clean, so that you didn't know who Donald Trump was. One day, you met him and started a conversation with him. Do you think your first impression of him would be, "That is a man with a lot of self-confidence who knows what he wants"?

People who try to convince other people that they are "a somebody" by being a show-off, rude, arrogant, or aggressive will only prove they are not confident.

People who "bad mouth" others, giving negative remarks about people behind their backs, are not positive and make a bad impression.

That's why I called this book *Get Happy and Confident*. When you are and act happy, confidence follows. You'll be more likely to take risks with a smile on your face and have fun in life.

The Power of Food

Why You Are What You Eat

An important solution in overcoming my panic attacks was food (part of the success behind my ilovepanicattacks.com program is the discussion of all the ingredients that make people feel anxious).

After I overcame panic attacks, I started to dig deeper. I knew there had to be a link between my state of mind, my happiness, and the food I was eating.

I want to stress that I am not a doctor or an expert in nutrition. I'm a guy who has done testing on himself, again and again, to find out how get the most out of life, and food was an important part.

What is happiness? What is confidence? It's a feeling. What is a feeling? It's the way your body feels and the way you feel on the inside.

We all know that food defines how much we weigh and how we look on the outside. That alone might decrease or increase self-confidence. What might be new to you is that you can change how you feel as well.

Carl was a great man. He was friendly, his colleagues loved him, and he was happy in life.

He had been working for the same firm for over ten years, his career was progressing, and he had a great family life.

Things started to change. A major coffee chain where you can spend a lot of bucks opened next to his office. Carl had never drunk coffee before.

One day, he was invited by some colleagues to have lunch there, and Carl drank his first coffee and ate some pastries. This was weird because Carl avoided foods with a high glycemic index or a lot of sugar, and when he could, he avoided gluten.

The next day, while passing that coffee shop, he smelled the fresh coffee, and he had to go in to buy something with a weird Italian-ish name. And hey, he couldn't skip getting some pastries, could he?

Carl's colleagues began to see a difference in his behavior. He was more nervous, anxious, and irritable. He could go into a rage out of nowhere, and that was totally new for Carl.

At home, things were changing. He was mad at the children and unfriendly toward his wife. He didn't want to go out and preferred to sit in front of the TV all the time. He was always sleepy but had a hard time falling asleep at night.

He gobbled down a tall coffee and some pastries every day. He was addicted and didn't see anything wrong with it. Why should he? Everyone was doing it, right? How bad could it be?

When Carl's wife urged him to do something to fix his situation, he found my website and contacted me. I asked him some questions about the changes in his life, and it didn't take me long to pinpoint the problem: coffee and sugar. I didn't have scientific proof for why these foods were making him mad (I did know that coffee can make you a lot more anxious and nervous) but asked him to skip those foods.

It was hard for him. He realized how addicted he was when he had to pass by that great smell of coffee and when he had to enter the office with nothing but a bottle of water in his hand.

Two weeks later, the old Carl was back. He was happy, calm, slept better, and didn't lose his temper. The only thing he had changed was drinking coffee.

When I wrote this book, I had more than five thousand active clients who were following one of my CD courses. I wanted to stay involved, and it was taking a lot of my energy.

Because I was so tired, it was difficult to feel happy. Are you ever really happy when you are tired? I think being tired excludes happiness.

I slept a healthy seven to eight hours every night, so I did not want to add extra sleep. I didn't have time for that.

I looked at my food. At first, I started to eat more carbohydrates—oatmeal, pasta, etc. These foods gave me an energy spike, but I was even more tired soon afterward.

I stumbled upon *The Paleo Diet,* written by Dr. Loren Cordain. The basics were simple: I had to exclude all gluten and grain in any form, including rice and corn.

I decided to give it a try and found it especially hard in the morning. What was I supposed to eat? I started to make salads with avocado and shrimp.

I decided to skip all sugar, in any form, and I especially stayed away from sugar replacements like aspartame.

About a week after starting this diet, I felt different. When I woke up, I had immediate energy. I didn't even need my alarm clock. I felt good!

After lunch, I didn't have an "afternoon dip," and my energy remained constant. I felt good the entire day, and I was smiling all the time.

I felt a kind of joy coming from the inside, and on the outside, my body started to change as well. I read *The Primal Blueprint* by Mark Sisson. This book advocates the same lifestyle as the Paleo Diet in general but adds related activities like going for walks instead of jogging.

My muscles started to form quicker than ever before, and I wasn't even going to the gym! I was doing exercises, but they took five minutes a day (I did a couple of pull-ups or pushups, things like that).

My body was happy, and I started to radiate energy.

Could you give it a try? Would you be willing to cut out sugar and gluten for four weeks? It may be hard at first. I read that the body becomes addicted to sugar quicker than it would to cocaine[7]. For more information, read *The Paleo Diet* or *The Primal Blueprint.*

For me, it's easier to feel good, to be healthy, happy, and confident when I don't attack my body with substances like sugar and gluten. You may want to try this as well.

---

[7] Magalie Lenoir, Fuschia Serre, Lauriane Cantin, Serge H. Ahmed. University Bordeaux 2, Université Bordeaux 1, CNRS, UMR 5227, Bordeaux, France

What You Should Remember after This Chapter:

✓ What you eat and drink defines the outside of your body, but it also greatly defines how you feel.

What You Should Try after This Chapter:

✓ Monitor how you feel. When you feel tired or depressed, jot down what you eat and drink that day. When you feel especially happy, do the same. After a couple of weeks, compare notes. You'll start to find the foods that give you a great feeling and those that don't. The list will be different for every person. (Alcohol, for instance, makes some people happy and makes other people sad or mad).

Forget about Yesterday

Yesterday Is Gone and Done

Mike is an accountant who works for a large international firm in New York. Mike is supposed to be happy and leading a good life, but he isn't.

When Mike was thirteen, he was picked on at school. He was overweight, wore glasses and looked "funny". Some would say he was a big nerd, and that's what they told him, over and over.

He didn't have many friends and, as a consequence, he hid himself in his school books. The positive consequence was that he had great grades.

At twenty-four, he kissed a girl for the first time, but it would be the last time for many years to come. He couldn't talk to girls. He was afraid to walk up to them, didn't know what to say, and felt inferior, so his love life was nonexistent. He couldn't say that the blind dates his sister set him up with were anything close to a love life.

At work, things were good but not great. Mike was passed by for many promotions because he was afraid to stand out, to show himself to his superiors. He was afraid to lead or to upset anyone. He was a nice guy, but he always finished last.

The only person who really respected and loved Mike was his goldfish, Blackie, the black type with the big eyes. They spent many Friday and Saturday evenings together, watching TV and having one-way conversations.

One morning, he woke up and felt a void. One of his friends was getting married that day to a great girl. Mike started to go over his life—to look back and to look ahead.

Where did it go wrong? Why was his life so dull? Was it because he had been picked on? Was it because of the wedgies?

He thought it was, found my website, and asked for my help.

Seven months later, yes, it did take some time, Mike was a changed man. Here is what I told him and what happened.

Are there things that happened in the past that still control your everyday life and your future?

Here's an interesting parable about two monks and a beautiful woman.

Two monks were making a pilgrimage to venerate the relics of a great saint. During the course of their journey, they came to a river where they met a beautiful young woman—an apparently worldly creature, dressed in expensive finery and with her hair done up in the latest fashion. She was afraid of the current and afraid of ruining her lovely clothing, so she asked the brothers if they might carry her across the river.

The younger and more exacting of the brothers was offended at the idea and turned away in disgust. The older brother didn't hesitate, quickly picked the woman up on his shoulders, carried her across the river, and set her down on the other side. She thanked him and went on her way, and the brother waded back through the waters.

The monks resumed their walk, the older one in perfect equanimity and enjoying the beautiful countryside, while the younger one grew more and more brooding and distracted, so much so that he could keep his silence no longer. He burst out, "Brother, we are taught to avoid contact with women, and there you were, not just touching a woman but carrying her on your shoulders!"

The older monk looked at the younger with a loving, pitiful smile and said, "Brother, I set her down on the other side of the river. You are still carrying her."

The more you carry in your "backpack" from the past, the more you'll be dragged back.

Children know how to enjoy life, but as they age, as their backpack gets bigger, they lose self-confidence and happiness, and they slow down.

Now why on earth is that necessary?

And why does this happen? It's simple: as they become adults, they still live in the past or try to live in the future.

That's funny, because the only time we can act upon is the now. *Now* is all we have.

Happy, self-confident people know this. They enjoy the now.

Stephen Leacock said it well:

The child says, "When I am a big boy."

The big boy says, "When I grow up."

The grownup says, "When I get married."

The married say, "When I'm retired."

They all forget to live now. Life is not tomorrow, it wasn't yesterday, it's now. This is one of the first things to remember in life.

Thinking about the bad moments in the past will take your smile away.

Let's look at Mike again. Because he was called a "nerd" when he was thirteen, he always believed he was a nerd and behaved like one. He never got rid of his past until he met me, and he never said: "Today is a new day. Today I can be anyone I want to be, today I will…".

That wording is exactly what started a domino effect for him. I asked him to look at every day as practice for the next. Every day he should do something outside of his comfort zone. He should play and test.

This included finding out how people reacted to the more assertive and self-confident version of him. He had to "fake it 'til he made it," and that's exactly what he did.

Is something from your past still limiting your life— something that hurt or scared you, that you feel guilty about, or a feeling of failure? That event might be a shadow over the rest of your life, but it doesn't need to be.

Every day is a new day. Nobody can change the past, but what you do today can define large parts of your future. Let's get rid of what happened yesterday or before and see how we can change how you feel today and tomorrow.

If, like Mike, you had bad experiences in the past, there are a couple of ways to deal with them.

The easiest way is saying *and* believing that "whatever happened, happened." What didn't kill you can only make you stronger.

I've had to face many obstacles in my personal life. We all have them; it's a part of life and the sooner you except this, the stronger you will become.

Another way to reprogram the past is to reprogram your memory.

Did you know that if you keep repeating a lie to someone, after a while, you won't realize it was a lie? It will feel real to you, because you've vividly imagined it happening over and over. We'll use that to change how you feel about your past. Let me first add an interesting idea that Anthony Robbins taught me:

"Your mind does not know the difference between what is real and what you vividly imagine."

This is one of the reasons why nightmares can feel so real. To your body, it was real. This has been scientifically proven.

We can use a combination of these factors to reprogram things that happened and change the feelings that are linked to them.

Did something bad happen in your past that you still drag with you—people laughing, mocking you, not treating you with respect, or other events that might cause a serious drop in self-esteem?

When I was fourteen, I was a fragile boy with glasses, so I was the target of every bad boy in school. It didn't kill me and boy, did it make me strong. Those bullies are far from living the life I live now. What did I do to change my feelings around this and remove it out of my backpack of bad memories?

I changed the past.

Yes. That's what I actually did.

When I was in a relaxed state, while listening to relaxing music, I started to imagine a specific bad moment, and then I started to change it.

I could do that, because it was my imagination, and everything is possible there. I'm the director of the movie I create.

Let me give you a specific example. A guy who was twice as large as me once dragged me by my foot through a hallway in school. That wasn't one of my best moments.

I imagined how I kicked him and how he started to get weird pimples and other problems with his skin, how everyone started to applaud and support me.

Did that really happen? No, but because, I imagined this daily when I was in a relaxed state, I now believe it to be true. My memory believes this to be true, and when I think back, I start to feel strong instead of weak.

When you read this for the first time, I understand that you might be skeptical. I understand that it must seem ridiculous, but it works. Give it a try.

Your mind is playing tricks on you all the time, so why not use some of its powers to your advantage?

Let me repeat why this works:

- If you vividly imagine something, your mind does not know it's not real, because it doesn't know the difference between what is real and what is not.

- If you repeat a lie, your mind forgets it is a lie.

Try this technique when you feel bad about something in your past. Change what made you feel bad, using your imagination, and do it over and over again while you are in a relaxed state. Play with it and make a movie out of it in your imagination.

You can use relaxation music, or you can go to gethappyandconfident.com, subscribe to my newsletter (to get access to the members area), and download an MP3 version of a relaxation that I created that will guide you, for free.

There is another way to use this technique: become who you want to be.

Still using the combination of the two principles, when you vividly imagine yourself being happy, full of self-confidence and joy, you will start to feel that way in real life.

When I had panic attacks, I used my imagination and pictured myself speaking in front of a large audience with a smile on my face. I saw myself dancing on a beach with a lovely woman by my side. Because my mind thought those images were real, it increased my self-esteem more than ever before.

Try it for a couple of weeks. You'll be surprised at the changes you will feel.

As always this is something that might feel unnatural at first, but it can change you afterwards. Use any relaxation you want, or get the free relaxation MP3 at my website.

The fact that the mind doesn't know the difference between what is real and what is vividly imagined has been proven on multiple occasions.

In the brain, simulating an act is the same as performing it. We don't need to execute the actual act.

L. Fadiga conducted a study that was published in the *Journal of Neurophysiology* 73, no. 6 (1995)). Researchers monitored the activity of motor neurons in the brain (motor neurons are used when we want to move or act).

This motor system was excited when the study participants saw someone else make a certain movement with an object.

For instance, if they saw someone else grasp a cone and move it, the same neurons in their brain were activated, as if they were moving the cone (they weren't; they just sat and watched).

Scientists call this "mirroring," and I am using it throughout the techniques described in this book.

What You Should Remember after This Chapter:

✓ Forget about negative moments in the past. They are gone and unless someone invents a time machine, you cannot change it.

What You Should Try after this Chapter:

✓ Try the visualization and imagination techniques I described for changing the past and for changing who you want to be.

✓ Learn to feel their power, especially if you're not open to "that kind of thing." (I wasn't either, but doing so created great changes for me.)

Why So Negative?

It's All Because of Saber-Toothed Tigers

Why are we so negative? Some of my clients have asked me this question. "Yesterday I had negative thoughts? Is all lost now?"

Of course, all is not lost. We are built to be negative; we are not built to find the good.

Imagine traveling back ten thousand years, and you are walking in a nice forest. You're enjoying the chirping birds and the humming bees. The flowers are beautiful, especially those yellowish ones with a hint of orange. As you are enjoying them, one of those "flowers" jumps toward you and eats you. It was a saber-toothed tiger, and you didn't see it because you were enjoying the "flowers."

Humans who did not see this coming would not have survived. They would not be able to procreate, and their genes would not be passed on.

Whose genes were passed on? The person who walked in the forest, seeing the flowers but not enjoying them. It was the person who was alert and anxious. That person would have seen the saber-toothed tiger coming. That person would procreate and pass on the "mind your steps" message to his children.

This is a clear example of survival of the fittest. The brain looks for two things:

1. Good things (food, pleasure, items we enjoy)

2. Bad things (dangers, animals that want to eat us or something that will get us fired)

There are many good and bad things that cross our paths in life. Ten thousand years ago, imagine that we would find some great food, that's great, but there can be found more tomorrow. But it only took one saber-toothed tiger to put an end to it all.

The mind is programmed to look for bad things—to focus on them, think about them, worry about them. We notice the good things, but when there's something bad as well, that's where our thoughts go.

This was necessary for survival then, but today, we don't have to accept this. I hope the exercises in this book will help you to train your mind, to play with it, and learn to shift your focus to find the good.

Epilogue

I want to sincerely thank you for reading this book. I hope you enjoyed it *and* that you will read it again and again. Nothing will change if you read it once; a lot will change when you practice what I have talked about and implement the practices in your life.

If you liked what you've read and want more, you can subscribe to my free newsletter on gethappyandconfident.com where I share my newest findings.

It was an honor to serve you.

Geert

Made in the USA
Middletown, DE
10 August 2021

45774783R00075